Dalziel/Dalyell

by Iain Gray

WRITING *to* REMEMBER

79 Main Street, Newtongrange,
Midlothian EH22 4NA
Tel: 0131 344 0414   Fax: 0845 075 6085
E-mail: info@lang-syne.co.uk
www.langsyneshop.co.uk

Design by Dorothy Meikle
Printed by Printwell Ltd
© Lang Syne Publishers Ltd 2021

All rights reserved. No part of this publication may be reproduced, stored or introduced into a retrieval system, or transmitted in any form or by any means (electronic, mechanical, photocopying, recording or otherwise) without the prior written permission of Lang Syne Publishers Ltd.

ISBN 978-1-85217-785-0

Dalziel/Dalyell

MOTTO:
I Dare

CREST:
A dagger erect

TERRITORY:
North Lanarkshire, West Lothian

NAME variations include:
Dalyeil
Dalzell

Chapter one:

The origins of the clan system

by Rennie McOwan

The original Scottish clans of the Highlands and the great families of the Lowlands and Borders were gatherings of families, relatives, allies and neighbours for mutual protection against rivals or invaders.

Scotland experienced invasion from the Vikings, the Romans and English armies from the south. The Norman invasion of what is now England also had an influence on land-holding in Scotland. Some of these invaders stayed on and in time became 'Scottish'.

The word clan derives from the Gaelic language term 'clann', meaning children, and it was first used many centuries ago as communities were formed around tribal lands in glens and mountain fastnesses.

The format of clans changed over the centuries, but at its best the chief and his family held the land on behalf of all, like trustees, and the ordinary clansmen and women believed they had a blood relationship with the founder of their clan.

There were two way duties and obligations. An inadequate chief could be deposed and replaced by someone of greater ability.

Clan people had an immense pride in race. Their relationship with the chief was like adult children to a father and they had a real dignity.

The concept of clanship is very old and a more feudal notion of authority gradually crept in.

Pictland, for instance, was divided into seven principalities ruled by feudal leaders who were the strongest and most charismatic leaders of their particular groups.

By the sixth century the 'British' kingdoms of Strathclyde, Lothian and Celtic Dalriada (Argyll) had emerged and Scotland, as one nation, began to take shape in the time of King Kenneth MacAlpin.

Some chiefs claimed descent from ancient kings which may not have been accurate in every case.

By the twelfth and thirteenth centuries the clans and families were more strongly brought under the central control of Scottish monarchs.

Lands were awarded and administered more and more under royal favour, yet the power of the area clan chiefs was still very great.

The long wars to ensure Scotland's

independence against the expansionist ideas of English monarchs extended the influence of some clans and reduced the lands of others.

Those who supported Scotland's greatest king, Robert the Bruce, were awarded the territories of the families who had opposed his claim to the Scottish throne.

In the Scottish Borders country – the notorious Debatable Lands – the great families built up a ferocious reputation for providing warlike men accustomed to raiding into England and occasionally fighting one another.

Chiefs had the power to dispense justice and to confiscate lands and clan warfare produced a society where martial virtues – courage, hardiness, tenacity – were greatly admired.

Gradually the relationship between the clans and the Crown became strained as Scottish monarchs became more orientated to life in the Lowlands and, on occasion, towards England.

The Highland clans spoke a different language, Gaelic, whereas the language of Lowland Scotland and the court was Scots and in more modern times, English.

Highlanders dressed differently, had different

customs, and their wild mountain land sometimes seemed almost foreign to people living in the Lowlands.

It must be emphasised that Gaelic culture was very rich and story-telling, poetry, piping, the clarsach (harp) and other music all flourished and were greatly respected.

Highland culture was different from other parts of Scotland but it was not inferior or less sophisticated.

Central Government, whether in London or Edinburgh, sometimes saw the Gaelic clans as a challenge to their authority and some sent expeditions into the Highlands and west to crush the power of the Lords of the Isles.

Nevertheless, when the eighteenth century Jacobite Risings came along the cause of the Stuarts was mainly supported by Highland clans.

The word Jacobite comes from the Latin for James – Jacobus. The Jacobites wanted to restore the exiled Stuarts to the throne of Britain.

The monarchies of Scotland and England became one in 1603 when King James VI of Scotland (1st of England) gained the English throne after Queen Elizabeth died.

The Union of Parliaments of Scotland and England, the Treaty of Union, took place in 1707.

Some Highland clans, of course, and Lowland families opposed the Jacobites and supported the incoming Hanoverians.

After the Jacobite cause finally went down at Culloden in 1746 a kind of ethnic cleansing took place. The power of the chiefs was curtailed. Tartan and the pipes were banned in law.

Many emigrated, some because they wanted to, some because they were evicted by force. In addition, many Highlanders left for the cities of the south to seek work.

Many of the clan lands became home to sheep and deer shooting estates.

But the warlike traditions of the clans and the great Lowland and Border families lived on, with their descendants fighting bravely for freedom in two world wars.

Remember the men from whence you came, says the Gaelic proverb, and to that could be added the role of many heroic women.

The spirit of the clan, of having roots, whether Highland or Lowland, means much to thousands of people.

Meanwhile, many families proudly boast the heraldic device known as a Coat of Arms,.

The central motif of the Coat of Arms would originally have been what was sometimes borne on the shield of a warrior to distinguish himself from others on the battlefield.

Clan warfare produced a society where courage and tenacity were greatly admired

Chapter two:

Royal honours

Pronounced *Diyell*, 'Dalziel' and its spelling variants including 'Dalyell' and 'Dalzell' is a locational name relating to the former barony of Dalzell in present-day North Lanarkshire.

Derived from the Scots-Gaelic *dail-gheal*, denoting 'bright dale' or *dal-gheail*, indicating 'white meadow', there is, however, a rather more fanciful explanation of its roots.

This is that during the reign from 1214 to 1249 of King Alexander II – although some sources say during the much earlier reign from 971 to 995 AD of Kenneth II – a close kinsman of the king was captured and hanged by his enemies.

Offering a reward for anyone brave enough to recover the body, a warrior stepped forward and declared 'Dal Zell', meaning 'I Dare' and, accomplishing the deed, was rewarded with lands.

Fanciful although this may well be, 'I Dare' is nevertheless the proud motto of the Dalziels.

Bearers of the name appear to have been settled in Lanarkshire certainly at a period before

1259 when, in the now defunct form 'Daliel' the Baron of Daliel is recorded as having served at an inquest while, in 1288, in the redundant variant 'de (of) Dalyhel', Hugh de Dalyhel was sheriff of Lanark.

This indicates the Dalziels had become well established, holding as they did a barony and serving as sheriffs.

Further proof of their prominence is found in the infamous *Ragman Roll* of 1296 – an invaluable source for the early appearance of many surnames found in Scotland.

A Thomas Dalielle of the County of Lanark appears as one of the signatories to the roll – a humiliating treaty of fealty to England's conquering King Edward I, known as the Hammer of the Scots.

Reluctantly signed at Berwick by 1,500 Scottish earls, bishops and burgesses, the parchment is known as the *Ragman Roll* because of the profusion of ribbons that dangle from the seals of the signatories.

Scotland had been thrown into crisis ten years earlier with the death of King Alexander II and four years later of his successor, the Maid of Norway, who died while en route to Scotland to take up the crown.

John Balliol, the son of an English baron, was controversially enthroned at Scone as King of Scots in 1292 – fatefully for the nation they had asked the ambitious Edward I to arbitrate in the bitter dispute over the succession to the throne, and the hapless Balliol had found himself Edward's chosen man.

The Scots rose in revolt against the imperialist designs of Edward in July of 1296, but the ruthless monarch brought the entire nation under his subjugation little less than a month later, garrisoning strategic locations and demanding the signing of the *Ragman Roll*.

Oppression under the iron fist of English occupation did not sit well with the proud Scots and the patriot William Wallace raised the banner of revolt in May of 1297.

A charismatic leader and expert in the tactics of guerrilla warfare, he and his hardened band of freedom fighters set Scotland aflame – boosting the morale of their fellow countrymen as they inflicted a stunning series of defeats on the English garrisons.

This culminated in the liberation of practically all of Scotland following the battle of Stirling Bridge, on September 11, 1297.

But, defeated at the battle of Falkirk on July

22, 1298, after earlier being appointed Guardian of Scotland, Wallace was eventually betrayed and captured seven years later and brutally executed in London as a 'traitor' on August 23, 1305.

His execution only served to further inflame Scottish patriotism, however, and the cause of the nation's freedom was taken up again, this time under the inspired leadership of the great warrior king Robert the Bruce, who had been enthroned as king at Scone in March of 1306.

Among those who rallied to his banner and were present at his great victory at the battle of Bannockburn in midsummer 1314 was a Thomas de Dalzell.

It is possible this was the same Thomas, recorded as 'de Dalielle' thirty years earlier as a signatory to the *Ragman Roll* or, more likely, one of his sons.

In 1628, Sir Robert Dalzell, born c.1550, was raised to the Peerage of Scotland by King Charles I as 1st Lord Dalzell.

He died in 1636 while his son Robert Dalzell, 2nd Lord Dalzell, created Earl of Carnwath in 1639, became embroiled in the bitter wars between Crown and Covenant.

Also known as the Wars of the Three Kingdoms of Scotland, England and Ireland and of which the English Civil War formed a part, they were sparked off in Scotland during the Bishops' Wars of 1639 and 1640.

These had their origin in the widely unpopular attempt by Charles I to foist uniform religious practice between the Church of England and the proudly independent Scottish Kirk, through the introduction into Scotland of the Episcopal Book of Common Prayer.

This acted as a catalyst for the signing on February 28, 1638 of the *National Covenant* – a document as important to Scottish history as the equally famed *Declaration of Arbroath* of 1320.

Described as 'the glorious marriage day of the kingdom with God', the Covenant renounced Roman Catholic belief, pledged to uphold the Presbyterian religion and called for free parliaments and assemblies.

First signed at Edinburgh's Greyfriars Kirk by nobles, barons, burgesses and ministers, it was subscribed to the following day by hundreds of common folk.

Copies were made and dispatched around the

country and received the enthusiastic support of thousands more – with its adherents becoming known as Covenanters.

This led to a civil war that raged between Covenanters and Royalists in Scotland from 1638 until 1649, when Charles I was beheaded on the orders of the English Parliament – whose military arm was Oliver Cromwell's New Model Army.

As a staunch Royalist, Robert Dalzell fought under the command of the charismatic James Graham, 1st Marquess of Montrose – but, captured after defeat at the battle of Philiphaugh, near Selkirk, on September 13, 1645, Robert was found guilty of treason and heavily fined.

His estates reverted to his son Gavin who, in order to clear off his father's massive debt, was forced to sell the family's ancient seat of Dalzell House and its grounds to a cousin, John Hamilton of Boggs – whose family retained the property until the death in 1952 of the 2nd Baron Hamilton of Dalzell.

What remained of the Dalziel lands in Lanarkshire, and also the earldom of Carnwath, were forfeited after the fifth earl fought for the Jacobite cause in the abortive Rising of 1715.

Built in the fifteenth century as a tower house

on lands acquired by the Dalziels two centuries previously, Dalzell House is a Category A listed building while its grounds, owned by North Lanarkshire Council and now a popular country park, are listed in the *Inventory of Gardens and Designed Landscapes in Scotland*.

Located in Motherwell, Dalzell House was extensively added to in the eighteenth and nineteenth centuries and, in the 1980s, restored and divided up for sale as private apartments that retain Jacobean-style detailing by the architect Robert William Billings.

Further reminders of the Dalziel presence in the area for centuries can be found in a number of place names and institutions that include Dalziel High School in Motherwell, Dalziel Rugby Club and Dalziel Park, near Carfin, and Dalziel Parish, a congregation of the Church of Scotland in Motherwell.

Chapter three:

Black Tam and the Devil

While one family of Dalziels was settled from the twelfth century in North Lanarkshire, a cadet branch named 'Dalyell' became established in the early years of the seventeenth century in West Lothian.

This was through Thomas Dalyell, an Edinburgh civic official who, benefitting from marital connections was able to purchase The House of the Binns – The House of the Hills – near Linlithgow.

Dalyell had been a wealthy butter merchant, importing the dairy product from Orkney to Leith where it was put not to culinary use but as axle grease.

He prospered further when he married Janet, a daughter of Lord Kinloss who, when King James VI of Scotland took up the throne of England in 1601 as James I, was appointed Master of the Rolls, a senior judicial position that also carried the responsibility of Keeper of the Great Seal of the Realm.

Keeping the lucrative sinecure and its

prerequisites very much in the family, he appointed his son-in-law as his deputy who, returning to Scotland in 1612 after having accrued great wealth, bought the manor and lands of The Binns from Sir William Livingston of Kilsyth.

He was the father of the Royalist general of the seventeenth century wars between Crown and Covenant Sir Thomas Dalyell of the Binns, 1st Baronet, and more notoriously known by those Covenanters he persecuted as 'Black Tam', or 'Bluidy (Bloody) Tam'.

Born in 1615, the fervent Royalist is said to have first taken up arms at the age of 13 while, on hearing of the execution in January of 1649 of King Charles I at the hands of English Parliamentarians, he vowed as an act of penance for their disloyalty never to shave his beard off.

Joining the Royalist army with the rank of colonel, he fought at the battle of Worcester on September 3, 1651.

This was when England's 'Lord Protector' Oliver Cromwell's 28,000-strong New Model Army defeated King Charles II's force of approximately 16,000, mainly composed of Scots such as Dalyell.

The king narrowly evaded capture – famously

hiding for a time in an oak tree – but Dalyell was among the 8,000 Scots taken prisoner.

Sir Thomas Dalyell of The Binns, 1st Baronet (1615–1685) – 'Black Tam', or 'Bluidy (Bloody) Tam'

Confined in the Tower of London, the redoubtable Tam managed to escape after only a few months and, with a price on his head, fled to Russia and entered the military service of Tsar Alexis I.

Fighting with great distinction in the Russo-Polish War, he returned to British shores on the Restoration of Charles II in 1660.

Following the Restoration, the death knell for the Covenanting movement was sounded when the Recissory Act was passed, declaring the National Covenant illegal, and Dalyell was appointed commander-in-chief in Scotland with the rank of lieutenant-general.

Episcopal rule was foisted on the Scottish Church, and all ministers who refused to adhere to this new order were deprived of their parishes.

Along with their congregations, many literally took to the hills, preaching at open-air meetings known as conventicles.

Lookouts were posted to keep a wary eye out for the approach of government troops and justice was executed on the spot for those unfortunate enough to fall into their hands.

Dalyell soon earned his notorious sobriquets of 'Black Tam' and 'Bloody Tam' through his brutal suppression of the Pentland Rising that culminated in the defeat of Covenanting rebels at the battle of Rullion Green, Midlothian, on November 28, 1666.

The rising had sparked off some weeks earlier in St John's Town of Dalry, Kirkcudbrightshire, when an elderly and infirm man was savagely beaten by troops for refusing to pay a fine levied for non-attendance at government-approved church services.

Passions were inflamed and a force of mainly ordinary citizens gathered and was steadily added to as it progressed through Dumfries and Galloway, Ayrshire, Lanarkshire and then on to Colinton, near Edinburgh, preparatory to the submission of a petition of protest to the Scottish parliament.

But a combination of news that the petition would not be favourably received, disunity in the ranks and atrocious weather led to plummeting morale and desertions from the 3,000-strong Covenanting force.

Commanded by the professional soldiers Major Joseph Learmont and Colonel James Wallace, the small band was cut to pieces by Dalyell and his sabre-wielding dragoons.

Those who were captured and not summarily despatched were later savagely treated – some tortured with the leg-crushing iron device known as the 'boot' – and others hanged, drawn and quartered.

But it should also be pointed out there is evidence Dalyell had shown mercy to a number of women and children who had been camp followers, and that the slaughter had been at the behest of his superior the Duke of Lauderdale.

In 1681, as the flames of rebellion still burned, Dalyell staged a grand muster in the grounds of The Binns to raise the Royal Regiment of Scots Dragoons – later known as the Royal Scots Greys and, following its amalgamation in 1971 with the Prince of Wales Dragoon Guards, the Royal Scots Dragoon Guards.

He died in 1685, while many legends attach to him – including that it was his habit to while away the evenings at The Binns by playing cards with the Devil, who invariably won.

But on one occasion Tam won and the Devil, infuriated, threw the marble table on which they played at him – but he missed his target and it ended up in the depths of a pond.

The pond was drained about 200 years later and the table recovered and placed in the entrance hall to The Binns – where it can be seen to this day along with other artefacts including the very cards with which Dalyell is said to have played with the Devil and his riding boots.

Set in 200 acres of parkland, The Binns was given to the National Trust for Scotland in 1944, with a proviso that the right of the family to reside there was retained.

One particularly famous twentieth century resident was Sir Thomas Dalyell of The Binns, 11th Baronet, more popularly known as the Scottish Labour Party politician and frequent thorn in the flesh of government Tam Dalyell.

Born in Edinburgh in 1932 but raised in The Binns – his family home through his mother Nora Dalyell – his father was Gordon Loch, a colonial civil servant.

Both he and his father took the Dalyell surname in 1938 while Tam, having inherited the baronetcy, never used his title.

Educated at Edinburgh Academy, Eton and King's College, Cambridge, he trained as a teacher and taught for a time at Bo'ness Academy, in the local authority area of Falkirk, before entering politics.

Labour MP (Member of Parliament) for West Lothian from 1962 to 1983 and for Linlithgow from

1983 to 2005, he was an early opponent of devolution for Scotland and posed what became known as the 'West Lothian question' – on whether non-English MPs should be able to vote on specifically English-only matters if devolution was granted.

Voting against his own government on no fewer than 100 times in 1978-79 over policy matters on which he strongly disagreed, he was also a highly vocal opponent of British military action during the Falklands War of 1982 and in particular the torpedoing and sinking of the Argentinean light cruiser *General Belgrano*, with the loss of 323 lives.

Opposed to the Gulf War and the invasion of Iraq in 2003, he accused Labour Prime Minister Tony Blair of war crimes.

Father of the House (of Commons) from after the 2001 general election until he stood down from Parliament in 2005, he died in 2017.

The author of books including his aptly titled 2001 autobiography *The Importance of Being Awkward* and, a year before his death, *The Question of Scotland – Devolution and After*, through his marriage to Kathleen Dalyell (née Wheatley), he was the father of the lawyers Gordon Wheatley Dalyell – who succeeded him as 12th Baronet – and Moira Dalyell.

Chapter four:

On the world stage

In the world of art, The Brothers Dalziel was an English family business of pre-eminent nineteenth century wood engravers whose artistic skills were used in the illustration of a range of books, newspapers and magazines.

Born respectively in 1815, 1817, 1822 and 1823, they were Edward, George, John and Thomas Dalziel, while their sister Margaret was born in 1819.

In an age that pre-dated photographic illustration, their art was in high demand and they became noted in particular for engravings used to illustrate John Bunyan's *Pilgrim's Progress* and, in 1862, Edward Lear's *Book of Nonsense* and also a number of works by Charles Dickens.

Artists they worked with include James McNeill Whistler and the Pre-Raphaelite Brotherhood group Dante Gabriel Rossetti, John Everett Mills and William Holman Hunt.

George Dalziel died in 1902, his brother Edward in 1905 and Thomas in 1906, while a collection of their work is now exhibited at the Victoria and Albert Museum, London.

From art to medicine, Thomas Kennedy Dalziel, better known as **T. Kennedy Dalziel**, was the pioneering Scottish surgeon born in 1861 in Penpont, Dumfriesshire.

The son of a farmer, he studied medicine at the University of Edinburgh and, after graduating in 1883, undertook further studies in Vienna and Berlin with his specialisms experimental surgery and pathology.

Joining the surgical staff of Glasgow's Western Infirmary in 1889 and, two years later, of the city's Royal Hospital for Sick Children, he also lectured in anatomy and became professor of medical jurisprudence and surgery at Anderson's College, forerunner of the University of Strathclyde.

Knighted for his services during the First World War as a member of the advisory council to the director-general of the Royal Army Medical Corps, he made a number of significant contributions to medical literature – particularly in the field of abdominal surgery.

One of the most important is his classic paper on the then little-understood disease *chronic interstitial enteritis* – now better known as Crohn's disease.

Regarded as the first to have drawn medical attention to the condition, he died in 1924.

Born of Scottish roots in 1881 in Newtown, New South Wales, **Elsie Jean Dalyell** was the eminent Australian medical doctor and pathologist who, in 1909, became one of the first women to graduate with a first class honours degree from the University of Sydney.

Completing a Master of Surgery a year later, she specialised in pathology and, in 1912, became the first Australian woman to receive a Beit Memorial Fellowship for Medical Research.

This took her to London, where she completed research at the Lister Institute of Preventive Medicine into gastroenterology in children.

During the First World War, she played a leading role in managing an outbreak of typhus in Skopje, Macedonia while later, serving with the Scottish Women's Hospitals for Foreign Service and the Royal Army Medical Corps, she was stationed at various times in a number of other theatres of battle.

The recipient of an OBE at the end of the war, she returned to her native land in 1920 before being appointed senior clinician with a research group in Vienna.

It was here that she carried out ground-breaking research into paediatric malnutrition, relating to diseases including rickets that afflicted infants.

She died in 1948, while Dalyell Street, in the Chisholm suburb of Canberra, is named in her honour.

One particularly unusual field of medical research was undertaken not by a doctor but an American professor of electrical engineering and computer science.

Born in 1927 in Santa Maria, California and a professor at UC (University of California) Berkeley, **Charles Dalziel** studied the effects of electricity on animals and humans.

This culminated in his 1956 book *The Effects of Electric Shock on Man*, examining the impact of different amounts of electricity on human subjects.

On a decidedly more domestic level, he was also the inventor twenty-five years before his death in 1986 of the ground-fault circuit interrupter, better known as GFCI and commonly found in kitchens and bathrooms.

Bearers of the Dalziel name have also excelled in the highly competitive world of sport.

On the football pitch, **Gordon Dalziel** is the

Scottish former striker and manager born in 1962 in Motherwell, North Lanarkshire.

Having played for Rangers, Partick Thistle, Ayr United, East Stirlingshire and Manchester City, he is best known for his time with Raith Rovers.

Scoring 202 goals in 378 appearances with the club, he is its record league goal scorer, winning the Scottish League Cup in 1994-95.

Also a football pundit, teams he has managed since retiring as a player include Raith Rovers, Ayr United and junior club Glenafton Athletic, while he was also director of football for a time with Airdrie.

On the rugby pitch, **John Dalziel**, born in 1977, is the former player with clubs including Gala, Melrose, Border Reivers and London Scottish.

Coaching posts he has held include head coach of the Scotland national under-20 rugby union team, head coach of the Scotland 7s and head coach of Melrose, while in 2019 he was appointed forwards coach for Glasgow Warriors.

From sport to enterprise and politics, a late nineteenth and early twentieth century newspaper tycoon and politician, **Davison Dalziel**, later more formally known as Sir Davison Dalziel, 1st Baron Dalziel of Wooler, was born in London in 1852.

Moving to New South Wales as a young man, he was employed for a time as a journalist before working in the United States in the management of a number of newspapers.

Returning to Britain in 1890, he set up Dalziel's News Agency and, in 1910, bought controlling interests in the London-based *Standard* and *Evening Standard* newspapers.

Also with interests in the General Motor Cab Company and the Pullman Car Company, he nevertheless found time to become actively involved in politics by serving from 1910 to 1923 as Conservative MP for Brixton.

Created a Baronet in 1919 and elevated to the peerage in 1927 as Baron Dalziel of Wooler, in the County of Northumberland, he died a year later.

Another British newspaper proprietor, **James Dalziel**, later more formally known as Sir James Dalziel, 1st Baron Dalziel of Kirkcaldy, was born in the Scottish village of Borgue, Kirkcudbrightshire, in 1868.

The son of a shoemaker, he excelled at school and, after attending King's College, London, worked for a time as a journalist.

Entering politics in 1892 as MP for Kirkcaldy

Burghs, he became an advocate of home rule not only for his native Scotland but also Wales and Ireland.

Having had a financial interest for some time in *Reynold's News*, he became its sole owner in 1914 and, three years later, also the *Pall Mall Gazette*.

Knighted in 1908 and raised to the peerage in 1918 as Baron Dalziel of Kirkcaldy, he died in 1935.

One colourful and influential figure in the world of fashion and style was the French-American socialite, magazine columnist and editor Diana Dalziel, better known by her married name **Diana Vreeland**.

Born in Paris in 1903, her father was the British-born stockbroker Frederick Dalziel and her mother the American socialite Emily Key Hoffman.

Moving to the United States with her parents on the outbreak of the First World War in 1914 and settling into New York high society, in 1922 she featured in an issue of *Vogue* style and fashion magazine – ironically, her future employer – in a roll-call of socialites and their cars.

Her picture caption read: "Such motors as these accelerate the social whirl. Miss Diana Dalziel, one of the most attractive debutantes of the winter, is shown entering her Cadillac."

In 1924 she married the banker and

international financier Thomas Vreeland, the couple moving to London five years later.

Entering the capital's social milieu, in the eleven years the couple spent there before returning to New York, she was presented to King George V and Queen Mary at Buckingham Palace, danced with the Tiller Girls and operated a high-end lingerie business near Berkeley Square.

Back in New York, she was hired by *Harper's Bazaar* magazine to write a column, later joining *Vogue* and serving as its editor-in-chief from 1963 to 1971.

An adviser to American First Lady Jacqueline Kennedy on matters of fashion, she was named on the International Best Dressed List Hall of Fame in 1964.

Also a special consultant at the Costume Institute of the Metropolitan Museum, New York, she died in 1989.

Portrayed by Juliet Stevenson in the 2006 film *Infamous* and, in the same year, by Illeana Douglas in *Factory Girl*, she was the subject of the 2012 documentary film *Diana Vreeland: The Eye Has to Travel*.